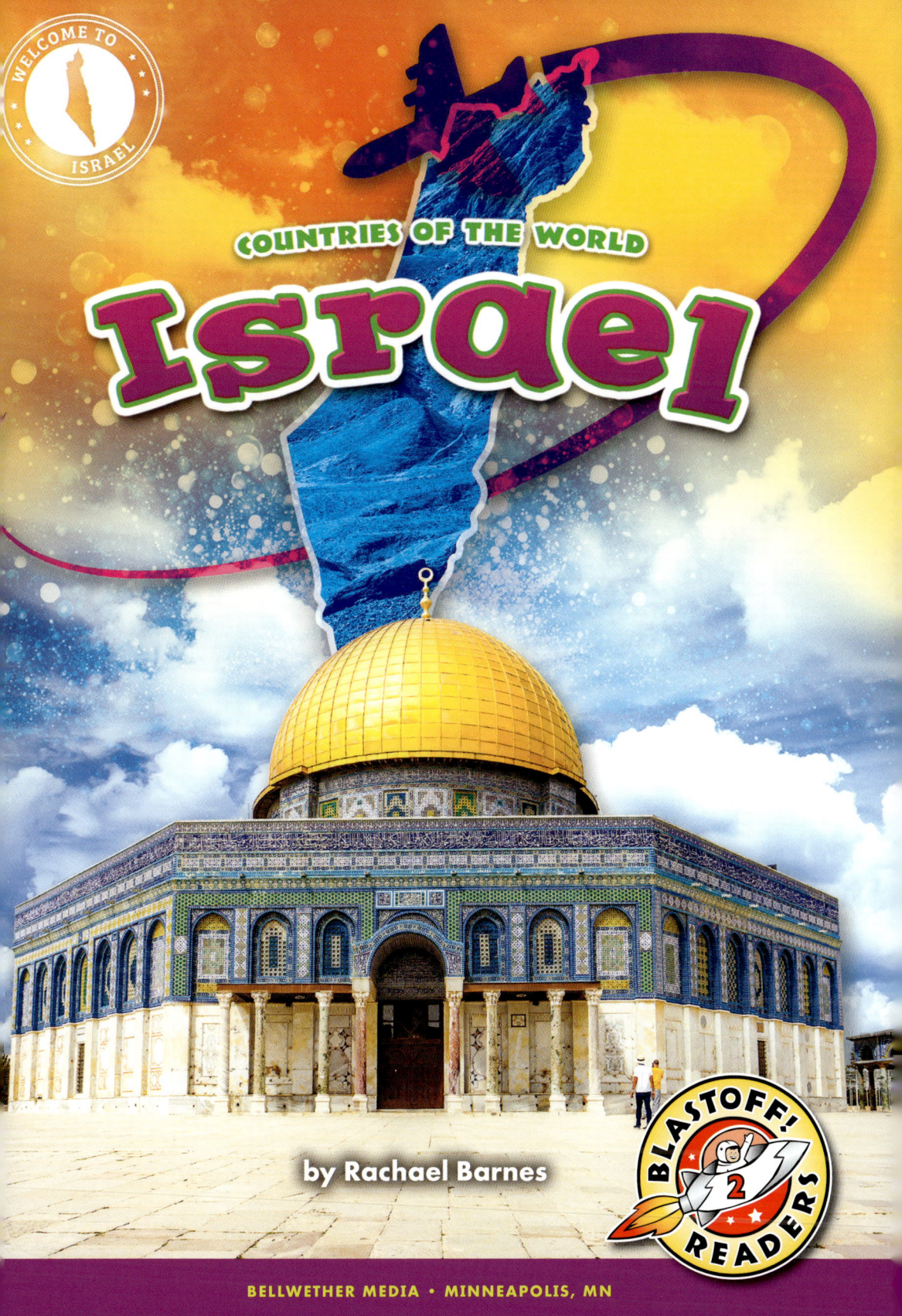

Blastoff! Readers are carefully developed by literacy experts to build reading stamina and move students toward fluency by combining standards-based content with developmentally appropriate text.

Level 1 provides the most support through repetition of high-frequency words, light text, predictable sentence patterns, and strong visual support.

Level 2 offers early readers a bit more challenge through varied sentences, increased text load, and text-supportive special features.

Level 3 advances early-fluent readers toward fluency through increased text load, less reliance on photos, advancing concepts, longer sentences, and more complex special features.

★ **Blastoff! Universe**

Reading Level

Grade K

Grades 1–3

Grade 4

This edition first published in 2023 by Bellwether Media, Inc.

No part of this publication may be reproduced in whole or in part without written permission of the publisher. For information regarding permission, write to Bellwether Media, Inc., Attention: Permissions Department, 6012 Blue Circle Drive, Minnetonka, MN 55343.

Library of Congress Cataloging-in-Publication Data

Names: Barnes, Rachael, author.
Title: Israel / by Rachael Barnes.
Description: Minneapolis, MN : Bellwether Media, Inc., 2023. | Series: Blastoff! readers: Countries of the world | Includes bibliographical references and index. | Audience: Ages 5-8 | Audience: Grades 2-3 | Summary: "Relevant images match informative text in this introduction to Israel. Intended for students in kindergarten through third grade"– Provided by publisher.
Identifiers: LCCN 2022044256 (print) | LCCN 2022044257 (ebook) | ISBN 9798886871333 (library binding) | ISBN 9798886872590 (ebook)
Subjects: LCSH: Israel–Juvenile literature.
Classification: LCC DS118 .B35 2023 (print) | LCC DS118 (ebook) | DDC 956.94–dc23/eng/20220923
LC record available at https://lccn.loc.gov/2022044256
LC ebook record available at https://lccn.loc.gov/2022044257

Text copyright © 2023 by Bellwether Media, Inc. BLASTOFF! READERS and associated logos are trademarks and/or registered trademarks of Bellwether Media, Inc.

Editor: Elizabeth Neuenfeldt   Designer: Gabriel Hilger

Printed in the United States of America, North Mankato, MN.

Table of Contents

All About Israel	4
Land and Animals	6
Life in Israel	12
Israel Facts	20
Glossary	22
To Learn More	23
Index	24

All About Israel

Jerusalem

Israel is small country in Asia. It is part of the **Middle East**.

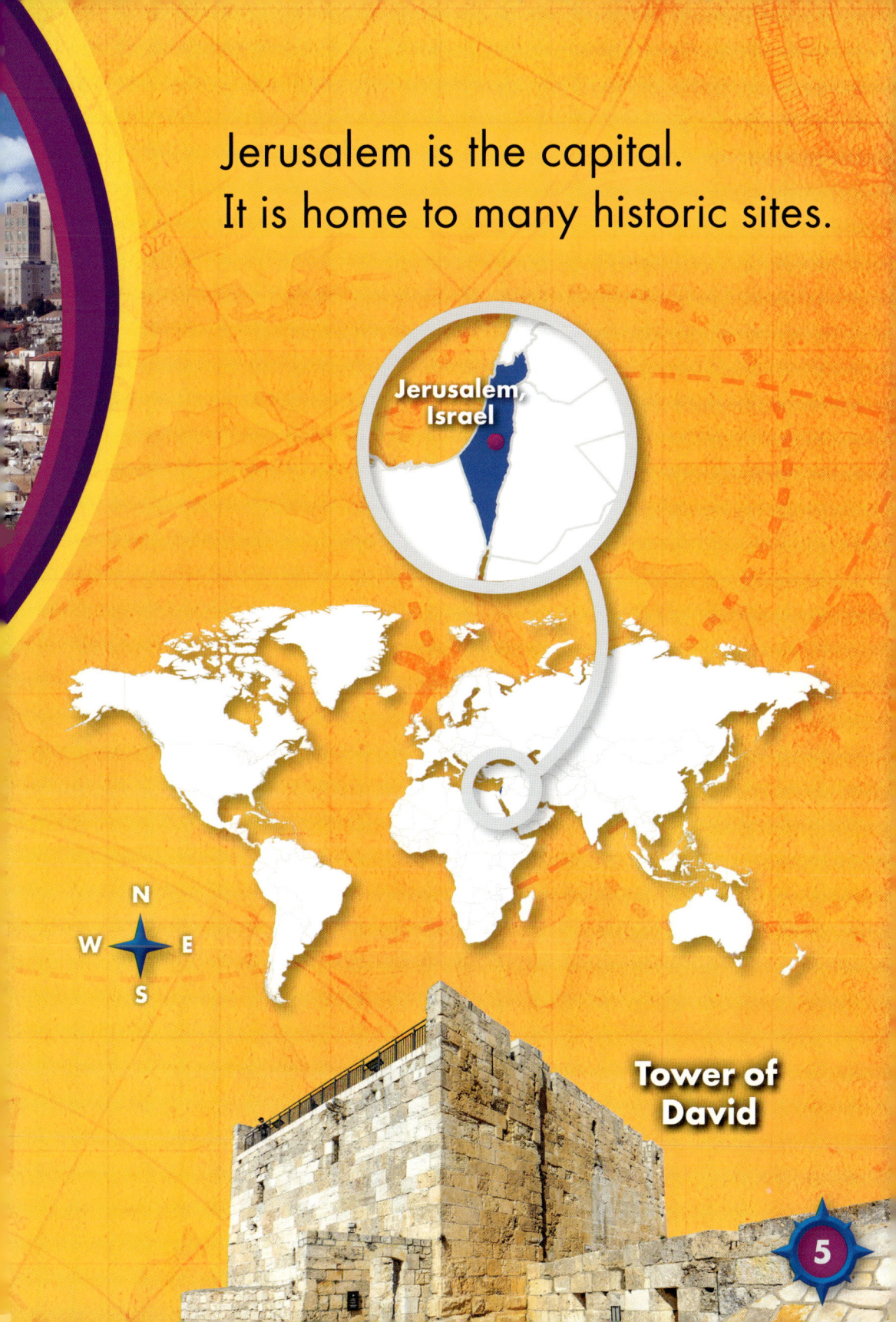

Jerusalem is the capital. It is home to many historic sites.

Jerusalem, Israel

Tower of David

Land and Animals

Beaches line Israel's northwest coast. They meet the Mediterranean Sea. Mountain **ranges** run from north to south.

Low valleys cut through the east. The Dead Sea fills the deepest valley.

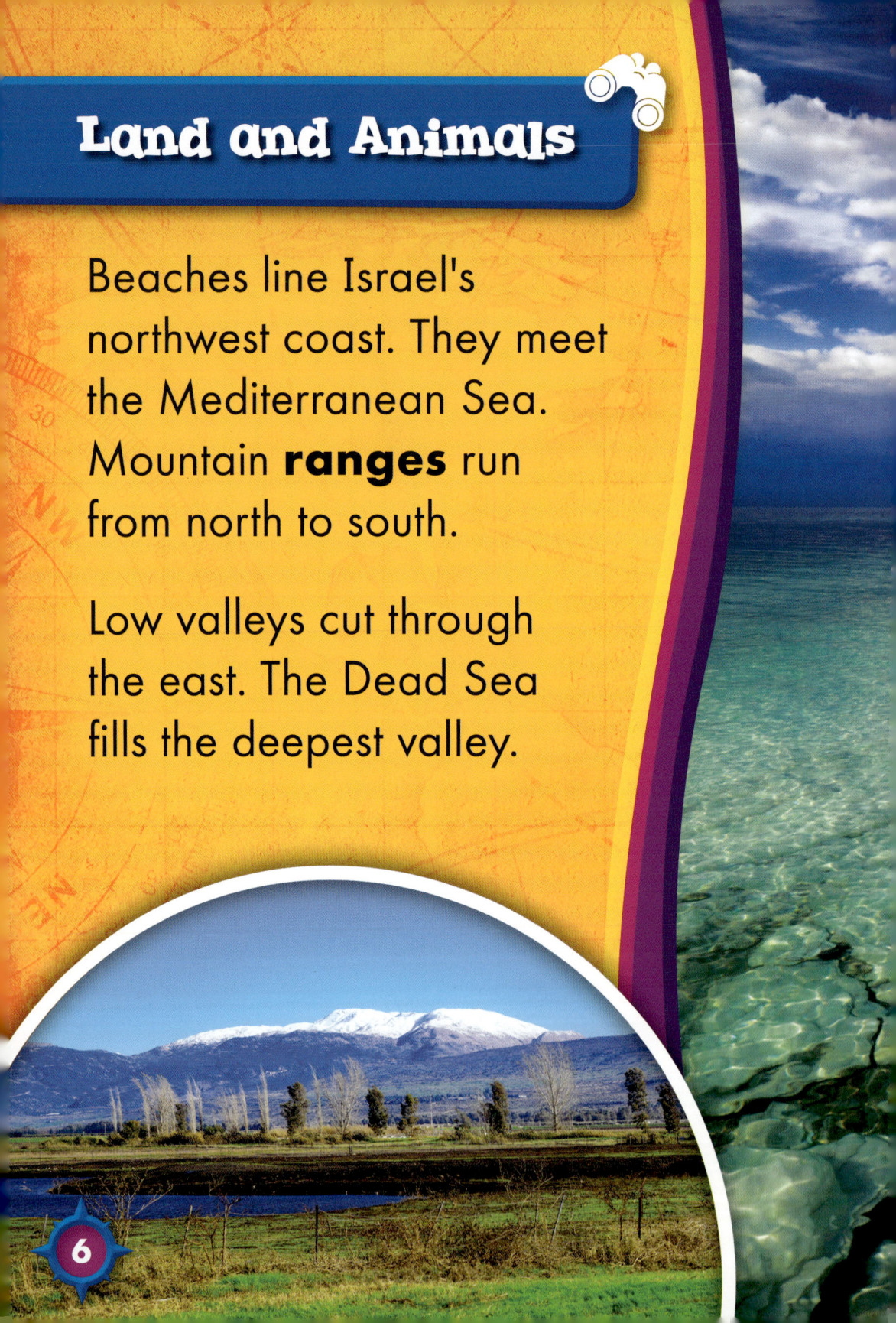

Dead Sea

Size: around 1,004 feet (306 meters) deep

Famous For:
- one of the saltiest lakes in the world
- Earth's lowest point on land

Israel has hot, dry summers. It is often sunny! Winters are cool and rainy.

The northwest receives the most rain. The southern Negev **Desert** is dry.

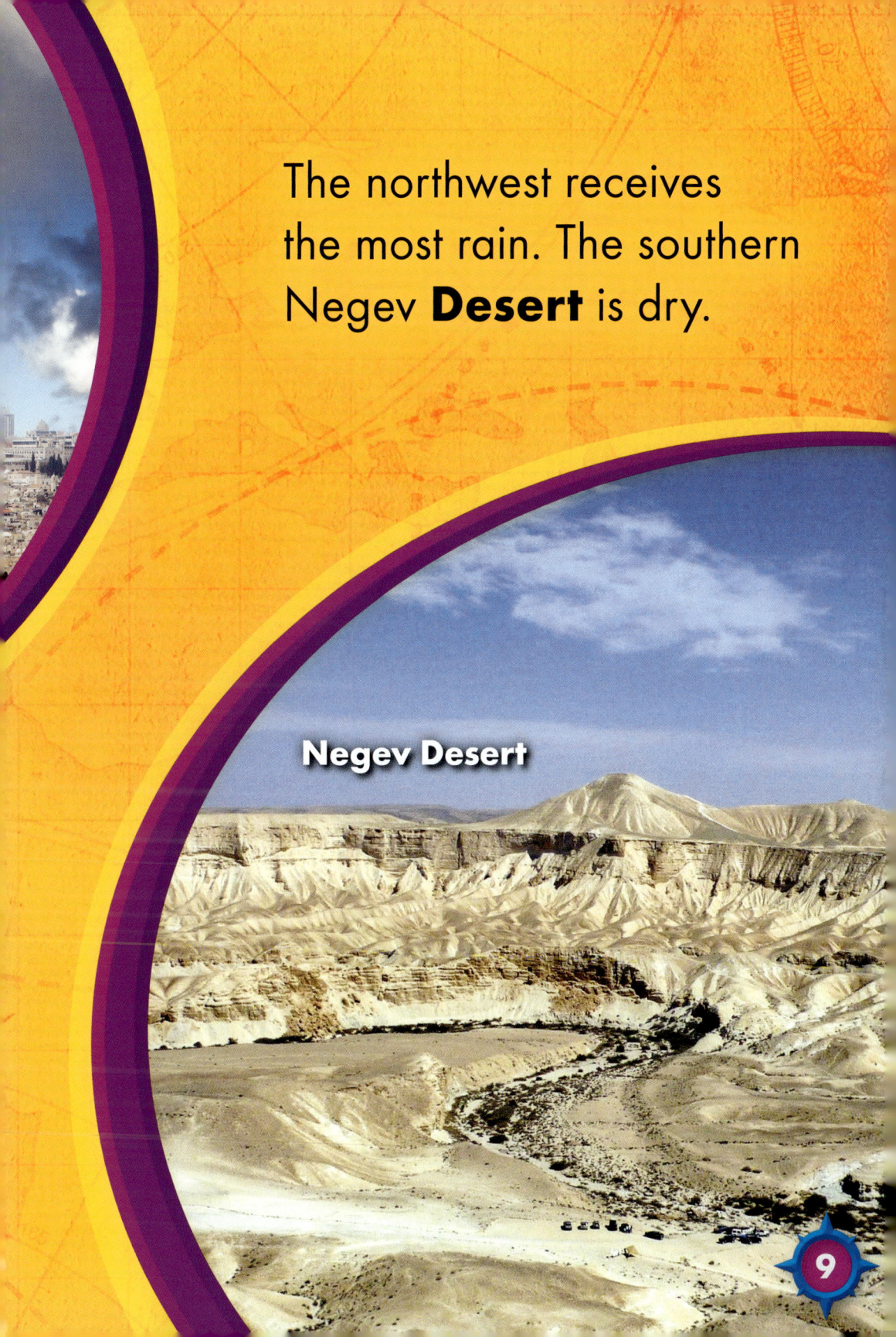

Negev Desert

Migrating pelicans rest near the Mediterranean Sea. Gazelles and hares munch on plants.

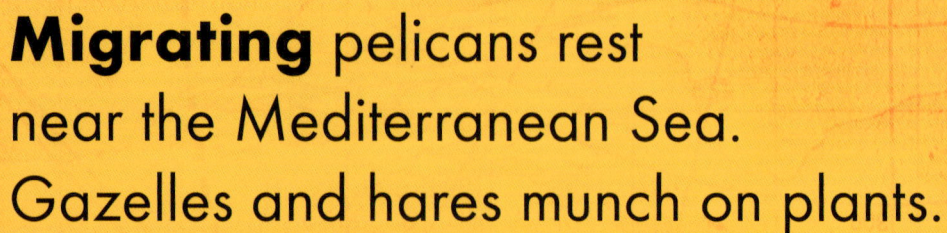

European hare

Animals of Israel

great white pelican

dorcas gazelle

rock hyrax

desert horned viper

Rock hyraxes live near the Dead Sea. Desert horned vipers slide through the sand.

Life in Israel

Most Israelis are **Jewish**. **Arabs** are a smaller group.

Hebrew is the national language. Arabic is also spoken. Nearly all Israelis live in cities.

Tel Aviv

basketball

soccer

Soccer and basketball are favorite sports. Some Israelis learn a **martial art** called *Krav Maga*.

People enjoy going out for meals and concerts. Families take trips to the beach.

Shakshuka is a breakfast **staple**. Falafel is a popular snack. *Krembo* is a tasty winter treat!

Israeli Foods

shakshuka

falafel

krembo

kugel

Many Jewish people eat **kosher** foods. Kugel is a favorite Jewish dish.

Hanukkah

Rosh Hashanah is the Jewish New Year. Every fall, families reflect and pray.

Winter brings Hanukkah. Families honor a **miracle** over eight days. Many **traditions** are honored in Israel!

Israel Facts

Size:
8,470 square miles
(21,937 square kilometers)

Population:
8,914,885 (2022)

National Holiday:
Independence Day (May 14)

Main Language:
Hebrew

Capital City:
Jerusalem

Famous Face

Name: Gal Gadot

Famous For: actress who is known for playing Wonder Woman

Religions

- Muslim: 18%
- Christian 2%
- Jewish: 74%
- other: 6%

Top Landmarks

Bahá'í Gardens

Dome of the Rock

The Western Wall

Glossary

Arabs—people who live mostly in the Middle East and northern Africa

desert—dry land with few plants and little rainfall

Jewish—related to people who came from the ancient Hebrew people; Jewish can also refer to people who practice Judaism, a religion that teaches a belief in one God.

kosher—accepted by Jewish law as fit for use

martial art—a sport or skill that first started as a way to fight or stay safe

Middle East—a region of southwestern Asia and northern Africa; this region includes Egypt, Lebanon, Iran, Iraq, Israel, Saudi Arabia, Syria, and other nearby countries.

migrating—moving from one place to another, often with the seasons

miracle—an event often believed to be from God

ranges—groups of mountains

staple—a widely used food or other item

traditions—customs, ideas, or beliefs handed down from one generation to the next

To Learn More

AT THE LIBRARY

London, Martha. *Gal Gadot*. Lake Elmo, Minn.: Focus Readers, 2021.

Server, Jessica. *Hanukkah*. North Mankato, Minn.: Capstone, 2022.

Spanier, Kristine. *Israel*. Minneapolis, Minn.: Jump!, 2020.

ON THE WEB

Factsurfer.com gives you a safe, fun way to find more information.

1. Go to www.factsurfer.com.

2. Enter "Israel" into the search box and click 🔍.

3. Select your book cover to see a list of related content.

Index

animals, 10, 11
Arabic, 12
Asia, 4
basketball, 14
beaches, 6, 15
capital (see Jerusalem)
cities, 12
Dead Sea, 6, 7, 11
food, 16, 17
Hanukkah, 18, 19
Hebrew, 12, 13
Israel facts, 20–21
Jerusalem, 4, 5
Krav Maga, 14
map, 5
Mediterranean Sea, 6, 10
Middle East, 4
mountains, 6

Negev Desert, 9
people, 15, 17
rain, 8, 9
Rosh Hashanah, 18
say hello, 13
soccer, 14
summers, 8
valleys, 6
winters, 8

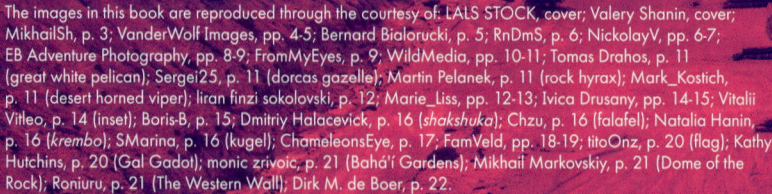

The images in this book are reproduced through the courtesy of: LALS STOCK, cover; Valery Shanin, cover; MikhailSh, p. 3; VanderWolf Images, pp. 4-5; Bernard Bialorucki, p. 5; RnDmS, p. 6; NickolayV, pp. 6-7; EB Adventure Photography, pp. 8-9; FromMyEyes, p. 9; WildMedia, pp. 10-11; Tomas Drahos, p. 11 (great white pelican); Sergei25, p. 11 (dorcas gazelle); Martin Pelanek, p. 11 (rock hyrax); Mark_Kostich, p. 11 (desert horned viper); liran finzi sokolovski, p. 12; Marie_Liss, pp. 12-13; Ivica Drusany, pp. 14-15; Vitalii Vitleo, p. 14 (inset); Boris-B, p. 15; Dmitriy Halacevick, p. 16 (*shakshuka*); Chzu, p. 16 (falafel); Natalia Hanin, p. 16 (*krembo*); SMarina, p. 16 (kugel); ChameleonsEye, p. 17; FamVeld, pp. 18-19; titoOnz, p. 20 (flag); Kathy Hutchins, p. 20 (Gal Gadot); monic zrivoic, p. 21 (Baháʼí Gardens); Mikhail Markovskiy, p. 21 (Dome of the Rock); Roniuru, p. 21 (The Western Wall); Dirk M. de Boer, p. 22.